MW01489750

Seeing IS BELIEVING

GEORGE E. VANDEMAN

Pacific Press Publishing Association
Boise, Idaho
Oshawa, Ontario, Canada

Edited by Bonnie Widicker
Designed by Tim Larson
Cover photo by Tom Rosenthal/Super Stock International Inc. ©
Type set in 10/12 Century Schoolbook

The author assumes full responsibility for the accuracy of all facts and quotations cited in this book.

ISBN 0-8163-0851-9

89 90 91 92 93 • 5 4 3 2 1

Contents

Chapter 1
Seeing Is Believing

Light. Color. Motion. Shape. Perspective.

There's much more to vision than meets the eye. Every time we open our eyes, we must translate an incredibly complicated mass of information into images that make sense. We see with our brains. And what we see can even help our minds to believe.

A lot of people today say they will believe only what they can see. As the saying goes, "Seeing is believing." Please try a little experiment with me for a moment. Picture in your mind our "It Is Written" set as it usually appears on the telecast. And try to imagine the scene if all the studio lights were suddenly turned off. Everything is in its place, just as it is every week. But that may be difficult to believe—if you believe only what you can see.

The railing around our raised platform is just as solid and real as ever. But to our eyes it appears hazy and a bit unreal—without one all-important element. The Bible at my circular table is just as solid and real as ever. But it doesn't quite seem so—without light.

Isn't it interesting that all these concrete, physical objects become real to us only because of something as insubstantial as light, something as spiritual, perhaps, as light. Plants take on a definite shape—in the light.

Wood shows its texture and form—in the light. The walls define the size of the room—in the light.

When we turn on all the lights, everything seems real. Now we can believe. Without light, we can't see to believe. Did you ever stop to wonder why? And did you ever wonder just how the human eye does see? Is it a camera, snapping away and sending pictures to the brain? Does it record scenes electrically? Let's look at just how light and our eyes work together.

When light strikes our eyes, it first hits the transparent cornea. The iris, located behind the cornea, controls the amount of light entering the eye by changing the size of the pupil—the hole in its center that appears black.

Once the proper amount of light has been admitted into the eye, it must be bent in order to focus. The cornea, because of its bulging surface, bends light sharply toward the center of the eye. The light then reaches the tiny lens, which is about the size and shape of a small bean. The lens consists of over 2,000 infinitely fine layers of transparent fiber.

This lens, unlike the lens in a camera, is pliable and can bulge slightly or flatten out. This changes the way light is bent and thus helps the eye to focus very sharply. Human vision is extraordinarily flexible. We can focus on objects a few inches from our nose and then switch instantly to a clear, sharp view of a distant star.

After being focused by the lens, light passes through the clear jellylike substance that fills most of the interior of our eyes. This vitreous humor is matched to the lens in such a way that it keeps light traveling in the same focused path.

Finally light hits the retina, a pink coating that

covers the back of the eye. The retina corresponds roughly to film in a camera. Packed into the retina lie what are called rods and cones. These photoreceptors contain light-sensitive pigments.

The rods and cones are a bit like having two kinds of film in a camera. Plump cones are most active in bright light. They give us full-colored, sharp vision. The slender rods are for dim light. Like highly sensitive black-and-white film, they create a monochromatic picture when little light is available. That is why color seems to disappear at night and we see basically different shades of gray.

About 130 million of these rods and cones are mixed together throughout the retina, occupying an area the size of a postage stamp. This enables us to switch with relative ease from vision in bright sunlight to vision in very dim light.

Our photoreceptors, the rods and cones, also perform another vital function. They transform the light they receive into signals, partly electrical and partly chemical. These coded signals are what will reach the brain.

To carry those signals, retinal nerve fibers are required. These fibers create a complex interconnected network that fans out over the retina. This data-collection system brings all signals together at one point. The nerve fibers are bunched together like a cable and pass out the back of the eye as the optic nerve.

Now things are just beginning to get complicated. The optic nerves from each eye crisscross in the brain. They somehow exchange information so that the images from two eyes can be coordinated into one stereoscopic field of vision. Then a new set of specialized nerve fibers picks up the signals and carries them to the visual cortex in the back of the brain. In this small mass of gray matter, the actual phenomenon of "seeing" takes place.

The billions of cells in our visual cortex are arranged in a number of layers. All these cells have highly specialized functions. Some send projections to other areas of the brain where memory and association occur. Most add, combine, exchange, and organize visual data in some mysterious way yet to be fathomed. The result is perception, a picture in the mind.

Clearly, seeing is no simple matter. The organs that produce sight are a marvel. Scientists tell us that the delicate engineering of the eye's cornea and lens makes the most advanced camera seem like a child's toy by comparison. The tiny rods and cones in the retina transform light into electricity and chemistry through processes the most sophisticated laboratory cannot reproduce. And finally, brain cells in our visual cortex synthesize countless bits of data into the miracle of perception—something no high-tech computer can come close to doing.

Engineering, chemistry, information processing—all are involved every time we open our eyes. All suggest that our eyes are marvelously designed. In fact, the more we learn about vision, the harder it is to ascribe all this ingenuity to chance. The eye all but demands a Creator.

We have to ask, Could the human eye have simply evolved from something simple to its present complexity? Let me tell you what Charles Darwin said about that. Darwin, you recall, is the man who first proposed the theory of evolution. But at one point he stated that the thought of how the eye could possibly be produced by natural selection made him ill.

There's a very good reason why the human eye is so distressing to the evolutionist and why it presents such a stumbling block to developing a consistent model of natural selection. The theory of evolution states that organisms change through natural selection. That means, for example, that strong, healthy animals are naturally selected to survive over weaker ones because they are better adapted to their environment. And slowly animals become better and better adapted. Beneficial changes are preserved; harmful changes are weeded out. All this, however, must happen over millions of years as a result of millions of tiny genetic changes. These mutations, it is believed, gradually accumulate and result in more complex living things.

Now here's the problem. The human eye is absolutely useless unless complete. It simply can't gradually evolve. There is no way that part of an eye could be beneficial to an animal. Natural selection would eliminate, not preserve, any partially developed eye organs.

The lens, which focuses light, would be useless without the retina, which senses light. All the light received would serve no purpose without the nerve fibers that carry signals to the brain. And these signals would be useless without the visual cortex, which interprets them.

Vision involves a complex interaction of nerves, muscles, fluids, glands, and brain cells. All must be perfectly integrated and balanced in order for us to see. Everything must be functioning or nothing functions.

So you see it is very, very difficult to imagine how something like the eye could develop gradually.

Thinking about it made Darwin ill. But it need not make us ill. The eye isn't just a baffling mystery. It is a wonderful work of art—if we understand it as the work of an Almighty Creator.

Seeing *is* believing. If we will only open our eyes to the wonder of vision, seeing can help us see the Creator God.

You know, it's interesting that this Creator is often spoken of in Scripture as Light. Light is a common symbol for the One who illuminates mysteries.

Listen to this exclamation in Psalm 27:1, NIV: "The Lord is my light and my salvation—whom shall I fear?"

When the psalmist feels a special need of God's presence, this is how he prays: "Let the light of your face shine upon us, O Lord" (Psalm 4:6, NIV).

And when God answers, the psalmist expresses his joy: "For with you is the fountain of life; in your light we see light" (Psalm 36:9, NIV).

When Jesus the Messiah arrived in Israel, He declared, "I am the light of the world." His disciples came to agree. Matthew wrote that, on the mount of transfiguration, he actually saw Jesus' face shine as the sun, and His garments become white as the light.

The apostle John called Jesus "the true light that gives light to every man" (John 1:9, NIV).

We have seen how vision and the eye point to a Designer or Creator. The Bible also tells us that light itself can point to Him. God is light. He illuminates. He warms. He makes things real. The symbol is pretty clear. But, you know, scientific discoveries about light have shown more about why it is an especially fitting symbol.

At first, light seems pretty simple. Look at any

light source and you see just a flood of white. But if you pass a ray of light through a prism, you see something quite different. The glass of the prism refracts or bends light and spreads the ray into its different wavelengths, causing the whole spectrum of color to appear.

It was through experiments like this that scientists long ago discovered that light actually contains all colors. The light we call white combines every color in the rainbow. In fact, color itself exists only through light.

Normally we think of an object's color as something it possesses, something painted on it. The redness of an apple seems a part of it, period. The color orange seems inescapably a property of an orange. But, in fact, the light falling on such objects is what gives them their color. When the colors in white light reach an apple, it reflects back to our eyes only one part of the spectrum, red light. The surface of an orange reflects back to us a different part of the spectrum, orange light. Light creates these colors.

If you look at a jar full of jellybeans in very dim light, they don't appear to have much color. But throw a strip of bright light on the beans, and their brilliant colors suddenly appear. Each kind of bean reflects back to us a particular part of the color spectrum in white light.

Yes, light creates color. Light fills our world with color. You know, I believe that says something about our Creator God. We've just looked at a few of the many places in Scripture where God is pictured as light, the true light that enlightens the world. Isn't it interesting to think that in God's light are all the colors of the rainbow?

Some people, unfortunately, have a rather narrow view of God and of His light. They see only white. They've grown up perhaps in a very strict religious environment. When they look at God, they can think only of restrictions. Faith becomes a kind of pale purity; all the gusto must be removed.

For too many people, religion seems to take all the color out of life. It limits them to just a few nice activities, a few pure pursuits. Everything must be a shade of white.

Listen, friends, I've got news for you. God isn't limited to one narrow slice of life. Our Creator has prepared a whole spectrum of blessings. It's time we stopped seeing only the white. There's much more to God's light than that. In His light a wonderful world of color opens up before our eyes.

Listen to what Jesus promised His followers: "I came that they may have life, and have it abundantly" (John 10:10, RSV).

Abundant life. That's what God, the true Light, is all about. Looking out at our world of color—how could we doubt it?

God's light fills our world with color. Look at the glittering leaves, shining back a hundred shades of green. The rippled sea, the peaceful blue expanse of sky. Flowers shouting out their wild array of reds, yellows, and purples. Shimmering waves of grain undulating in the wide fields. A glorious sunset ending the day with a splash of orange and magenta.

Just look at all the color. All the vivid scenes in our world. The rush of images. The spectrum split into a thousand hues and shades. Such abundant, such extravagant color!

The One who designed the marvelous complexity of

our eye also spreads before us a captivating display of color. And He does it all through His light, His abundant light.

Let me tell you about someone who collided rather dramatically with that light. A young Pharisee scholar named Saul lived in a world of black and white. He looked out at life through the Torah, the law. Everything related to rule or ritual in some way. Saul's mind was quick to grasp the complexities of Israel's laws. He had become an expert in interpreting and observing the many traditions of his religion. His life was carefully confined by actions that would maintain his ceremonial purity.

So Saul was not at all happy when a new Jewish sect arose that challenged his cherished traditions. The followers of the rabbi Jesus seemed nothing but troublemakers. Saul couldn't fit the dynamic movement of the Spirit into his narrow world of black and white.

Saul the scholar turned into Saul the persecutor. He heard about an active group of Christians in Damascus and decided to lead a party there to imprison them. Heretics were simply too dangerous to tolerate.

But on the way to Damascus, Saul was stopped dead in his tracks. A brilliant light suddenly flashed around him, and he was knocked to the ground. The zealous Pharisee heard a voice saying, "Saul, Saul, why do you persecute Me?"

And Saul answered, "Who are You, Lord?"

The voice replied, "I am Jesus, whom you are persecuting" (see Acts 9:4-6).

The bright light had blinded Saul. He was led by his companions into Damascus and there met a Christian named Ananias. From him, Saul learned much more about Jesus, the Light, who had interrupted his journey.

When Saul regained his sight, his world of black and white was gone forever. Saul the bigot had become Paul the apostle of God's grace. He had stepped into God's light and into a world of living color. There were no more narrow prejudices; all mankind was one in Jesus Christ. No more petty regulations; Paul saw the much wider duty of love. No more ceremonial restrictions; only the life of the Spirit counted now. In God's light, Paul saw that religion contained a whole spectrum of spiritual qualities: love, joy, peace, patience, gentleness, self-control.

When we read Paul's epistles in the New Testament, we can understand how broadened this former bigot had become. His heart was wide enough to love Philippians, Thessalonians, Ephesians, and Galatians. And he loved them all with a remarkable intensity. Paul was willing to give his life for them. Listen to his wonderful words to the Corinthian believers. To people having very serious moral problems he wrote: "I do not speak to condemn you; for I have said before that you are in our hearts to die together and to live together" (2 Corinthians 7:3, NASB).

What a contrast to Saul, the haughty Pharisee. What a difference God's wonderful light had made in his life. It can make the same difference in our lives today.

We don't have to live in a narrow little world of black and white. Religion doesn't have to be reduced to mere restriction. God's light can fill our lives with living color. He has promised to give us abundance.

And listen, we can trust Him to do that. Seeing *is* believing. We can trust the One who designed the intricacies of the human eye. No problem is too complex for Him to handle. We can trust the One who has spread such a wealth of color throughout our world. No life is too drab for Him to revitalize; no corner is too dark for Him to enlighten. Yes, we can trust this marvelous Creator with our whole lives. We can respond wholeheartedly to the prophet Isaiah's invitation: "Come, . . . let us walk in the light of the Lord" (Isaiah 2:5, NIV).

Chapter 2
Plant Prodigies

Exploring the local park or forest, most of us see only a mass of green, an assortment of nondescript leaves and branches spread before us. Little do we dream, on our Sunday afternoon strolls, that we are unwitting witnesses to architectural feats, chemical marvels, innovative aviation, and complex data processing. It's right here, if only we look closely enough.

Most of us use plants simply to grace our living rooms, add color to our porches, freshen up our offices. They're nice to have around, of course. Nice to have in the background. We don't notice them that much. We don't notice, for example, how much is involved in what appears to be a simple, common thing: a plant turning toward the light. We just kind of expect them to. They turn toward the light—naturally; they're attracted to it. Plants need sunlight to stay healthy, to grow. But *how* do they do it? And how do they manage that technological feat of turning light directly into energy?

To get inside plant life, let's first take a look up at the sky, up at a satellite orbiting the earth. Its measuring devices and transmitters operate on solar batteries. These cells convert sunlight into electricity—

small amounts of it anyway—much like a photographic exposure meter does.

Now this satellite, revolving and orbiting through space, won't always face the sun at the proper angle. In fact, its solar batteries would lie inactive in shadow much of the time. To avoid that, space scientists have developed a very complex tracking system. It measures the direction of the sun's beams, and then, by means of control motors, moves the solar cell panels to face the sun's rays for maximum exposure.

All this involves very complex processes: measuring the angle of light rays, interpreting the data logically, executing precise movements. The sun sensors, the computing system, the circuitry, and the control motors occupy considerable space in the satellite. Getting a solar battery to turn toward the light is no simple task. But all around us, plants are solving this intricate problem every day. And in many ways their technology is superior to ours. Yes, superior to the ingenuity of NASA's most brilliant scientists.

Much of the information shared in this chapter is based on a study of plants by science writer Felix Paturi. He called his work *Nature, Mother of Invention*. In this chapter we're going to see just how incredibly inventive Mother Nature is—by looking at plant prodigies.

Plants are masters of what is called "phototropism," the movement of plants when stimulated by light. They pack all the necessary mechanics—the means of measuring, interpreting, and moving—into one compact unit. And it's incredibly sensitive. A plant kept in a dark room for a day will react to a single flash of light two-thousandths of a second long. In a tree or bush, individual leaves bend and turn so that as few as possible are overshadowed and all take in adequate radiation. Plants have solved an energy problem that still plagues our industrialized world, and they've done it on a large scale. They use energy efficiently—and without hazardous wastes. Think about it. Plants have been producing refuse for thousands of years, far longer than factories. But they dispose of wastes without pollution. Their wastes are broken down in the soil to become food again. Production and decomposition cancel each other out. Everything is recycled. Such a well-balanced system can go on functioning indefinitely.

Sun power makes roses red, violets blue, and ferns green. Is it any wonder the psalmist was moved to write in praise of Jehovah: "He makes grass grow for the cattle, and plants for man to cultivate—bringing forth food from the earth" (Psalm 104:14, NIV)!

The psalmist saw a wise creator in the wonder of growing things. How much more should we see that now. Sunlight is a vital part of the miracle. And so is water. Let's look at how plants absorb it.

Say you live in an apartment on the sixth floor, about sixty feet from the ground. And let's say you and your family use forty gallons of water a day. It takes an extensive pipe system and a lot of pressure to pump those forty gallons, sixty feet up in the air. That's one reason you get those nice little bills every month.

But did you realize that a full-grown birch tree does that much work on a hot summer day? It gets forty gallons up to its branches and leaves every day, without electricity or gas or power pump. In fact, the tree itself needs supply no energy to do this. Everything is automatic.

When water evaporates from the leaves, it creates a

constant compensating suction of water below. The suction continues through twigs, branches, and trunk down to the roots.

This happens because the tree's "water pipes" are actually many, many microscopic tubes. No man-made suction pump has ever managed to pull water up more than thirty feet. Columns of water suctioned higher than this in ordinary pipes inevitably collapse. But the tallest of trees are able to suction up water to their uppermost branches—because of their "capillaries"—tiny tubes a few thousandths of a millimeter in diameter.

How true these words ring from Psalm 104:16: "The trees of the Lord are well watered, the cedars of Lebanon that he planted."

The trees that *He* planted, indeed, how ingeniously they are watered. But there's much more to plant technology and engineering. Did you know that plants are also extraordinary architects?

In the 1850s, architect Sir Joseph Paxton entered a competition to design the building that would house London's world exhibition. He longed to outdo his rivals with an epoch-making design. Paxton conjured up a building of gigantic dimensions which would have nothing heavy or clumsy about it; he imagined a structure that would produce the effect of lightness, even weightlessness. But the problem was, there was no way to construct such a building at the time. Large structures required massive walls to support them. There seemed no way to create the graceful, airy building Paxton had in mind.

But then he remembered a certain plant he'd worked with as a gardener in his youth: the royal waterlily. The floating leaves of this lily are huge, up to six feet in diameter, *and* very thin. But in spite of this, they're quite stable. They achieve this stability by a complicated strutting on the underside. Ribs radiate from the center of the leaf outward, splitting up into many branches.

The royal waterlily gave Paxton the key to making his architectural dream come true. He used a few main struts connected by many small ribs in his design. And he won the competition. The result: the Crystal Palace of the world exhibition, a smashing success. It proved to be a great turning point in architecture. The bold skyscrapers of steel and glass we see all around us today actually date back to that graceful, airy Crystal Palace, and, yes, back to the remarkable design of the royal waterlily.

Plants have also mastered the art and science of aviation. And they did it long before Orville and Wilbur Wright propelled their frail craft into the air. We see this most often in the way seeds navigate to suitable soil. If a tree dropped its seeds straight down, the seedlings would have to try to grow in the shade of the parent tree and would soon choke each other out. Seeds need to be transported away from the parent tree or plant, and this is accomplished in a variety of ways.

The common dandelion sends its seeds aloft by means of tiny parachutes. First the plant actually measures relative humidity, temperature, and wind velocity. It will release its seeds only when conditions are just right. A steady wind must be blowing, not just a brief gust; the air must be warm and dry—indicating that rising wind currents will prevail. Only then do the flying seeds let go and venture on their all-important journey. And these dandelion seeds, hanging under their parachutes like so many paratroopers, are able to travel remarkable distances.

Several other plants also transport seeds by means of parachutes. And what's very interesting is that these plants come from widely different botanical families. They are not confined to one species or genus; they are not one type of plant. Now this presents a real problem for the theory of evolution. It's one thing to assume that one plant group managed to evolve this ingenious parachute solution to the problem of seed transportation. That, in itself, takes a lot of faith. But to believe that a whole range of different plant types all developed this same amazing solution to a common challenge—that takes more faith than I could ever muster.

I hope you are beginning to see that behind all the ingenuity of plants solving technical problems lies one common denominator, one common source: an ingenious Creator.

From parachutes we move to gliders. The most interesting example is probably the winged seed of the tropical liana. It grows high up in the branches of its parent tree amid beautiful, shining green leaves. The liana seed develops two curved wings, transparent, gleaming, and very elastic. When the seed releases from the tree, it glides away in the breeze.

Coldly objective scientists grow eloquent when observing this bit of plant aeronautics. One professor described the liana glider in this way: "Circling widely, and gracefully rocking to and fro, the seed sinks slowly, almost unwillingly, to the earth. It needs only a breath of wind to make it rival the butterflies in flight."

Early aviation pioneers were also impressed with

the perfect flight of the liana seed. In building craft light enough to soar in the wind, stability was the key. Early flying machines kept falling apart. But the liana glider's gossamer wings were remarkably stable. And so two flying pioneers, Etrich and Wels, made use of the liana seed in designing a tailless glider. The craft that resulted in 1904 proved to be a milestone in aviation history, gliding for about 900 meters. Another technological marvel pointing to nature as the mother of invention.

Well, we've seen parachutes and gliders in the plant world; how about helicopters? The Norway maple seed is one example. It comes equipped with tiny curving wings. When the seed falls from the tree, air friction causes it to rotate quickly. It spins in a spiral path around the nut at its base. The effect is exactly the same as that produced by spinning helicopter blades. The rotation creates a complete circular surface which the wind can grip. And so, of course, the seed falls much more slowly, and the tiniest bit of wind can push it more than 100 yards. Aeronautics. Who would have thought that trees would lead the way? Who can fathom the creative Mind behind it all?

Think for a moment of a mainframe computer, one of the truly great feats of modern technology. Its ability to store and retrieve data, and to compute and sort and list is mind-boggling. Computers perform functions in a split second that would take mathematicians weeks or even months. These machines are real problem solvers.

And electronic computers are getting smaller and faster almost every day. Micro-electronics continues to develop tinier and more efficient chips and circuits. But as impressive as computer number crunching is, there's something even more impressive that I can hold in the palm of my hand, a tiny marvel that rivals all the information processing that a room full of computers can do. What is it? A common, ordinary seed.

Now some of you may be saying, "Wait a minute. I know seeds grow into flowers and trees, but doing the work of a computer? Isn't that taking it a bit far?"

Well, let's think about it. A single plant seed must contain all the plant specifications; all the information about its appearance and behavior has to be stored right in one seed. The size and shape and color of the plant, its reactions in heat and cold, light and shade, in drought or downpour—all must be determined beforehand in the seed. Now how many megabytes would be taken up in a computer just to program the color of a plant's flower? Or, say, to mathematically encode just the outward form of a tree? Think about programming in the exact geometric shape of leaves, buds, blossoms, fruit, bark, stems. We're getting into millions and millions of digital notations. Think about trying to program the chemical qualities of the cell sap, the disposition of various types of tissue.

And then try to figure out how to instruct the plant about survival techniques in various environments. How would you program in the remarkable range of adaptations we've talked about today?

Well, science writer Felix Paturi, for one, concluded that the storage capacity of a large modern computer would scarcely suffice for all this data. But it's all here, all that information and more is stored in each tiny seed.

Incredible computer. Do you want to look at the far horizon of high technology? You don't have to go to Silicon Valley. You don't have to go to MIT. Just dig up a seed burrowing into the ground. Here's information processing at its most mind-boggling.

Here is solid evidence for an infinitely wise Creator. I can't believe a seed is the product of natural selection or genetic mutation. Weak animals can be weeded out by natural selection. Genetic mutation can produce a few freaks now and then. But those blind processes don't invent computers this size. I'm sorry. That just isn't done.

If we can't see an incredibly ingenious God behind plant aviation and architecture and chemistry and the seed-computer, then something's wrong with our eyesight. Our Creator has solved a vast array of technical problems. He's created solutions that have inspired our greatest inventions. There's no question in my mind: God is a problem solver. He can solve any kind of problem.

In the book of Hebrews, Jesus is described as the One who "is able also to save to the uttermost," that is, save completely, perfectly, for all time.

That's the kind of confidence we can have in the one who causes plants everywhere to turn surely toward the light and bloom and bear fruit in those nurturing rays.

Perhaps you've been deeply wounded; perhaps you're bearing scars from traumas in the past or are nursing a very present bitter hurt. There is a problem solver ready to help the broken. Psalm 147:3 says of Him with simple eloquence: "He heals the broken-hearted and binds up their wounds" (NIV). Yes, that great Creator of the royal waterlily, that Architect of plant life, can be relied on to support us in our hour of need. He can build us up according to His ingenious blueprint.

Sometimes we may feel perplexed and lost. We need help in making important decisions. We can't always see very far down the road when faced with alternative paths. And sometimes there are just too many choices, too many voices clamoring for our attention and allegiance. We need clear direction; we need a sure guiding hand. And the Problem Solver comes to us and declares: "I will instruct you and teach you in the way you should go; I will counsel you and watch over you" (Psalm 32:8).

That's a great assurance to have, isn't it—coming from the One who sends maple and liana seeds off on their voyages, gliding, parachuting, helicoptering to a rendezvous with good soil? Certainly this Creator can be relied on to propel us in the right direction.

He is a master of working good out of evil. Let me show you one promise about this Problem Solver, found in Romans 8:28. This is from the Amplified Bible. It says: "We are assured and know that (God being a partner in their labor), all things work together and are (fitting into a plan) for good to those who love God and are called according to (His) design and purpose."

All things, all the things that happen to us, are fitting into a plan for good. God the ingenious problem solver makes all things work together for good. That's good news! That's the good news that is echoed in flying seed and strutted leaf and flower turning surely toward the light. God's creative powers are everywhere in evidence. And they all shout, God can handle your problems; He can deal with your challenges. He is able. His wisdom is wide enough. His strength is deep enough.

Chapter 3
Who Told the Honeybee?

Computers and rockets and dictionaries and planes are the product of genius and hard work. But the men who design them are the product of accident and chance. So we are told.

But did you know that the common honeybee, without even trying, can upset the conclusions of brilliant minds?

Just how much are you willing to attribute to the unlikely magic of the ages? If evolution happened, how did it happen? Would it be unreasonable to ask some specific questions—in one small area?

Come with me as we watch the fascinating activities of the common honeybee. I promise there will be some surprises—and a rather formidable dilemma for those who credit all creation to the supposed power of time to do in the past what it cannot do now!

Have you ever noticed that bees are incredible architects? The hive is a masterpiece of engineering, with rows and rows of six-sided rooms with walls of wax. The marble palace that we call the comb is built by young bees under seventeen days old. Yet each little room is the same size, six-sided, with each of three pairs of walls facing the other. The walls of the rooms are only 1/350th of an inch thick, yet so strong that one pound of comb will support at least twenty-five pounds of honey.

How do these young bees know that the hexagon has the smallest circumference, therefore requiring the smallest amount of building material? How do they know that hexagon cells are the best and most economical plan? Who told them? Yet they do it all without blueprints or drawing boards or protractors. And every cell is perfect—just the size to fit a bee!

How do they do it? They hang themselves up like a festoon from the roof of the hive. Or it may be in the hollow of a tree. One bee hooks onto the roof, and another bee hooks onto his dangling legs, and so on. These chains of bees grow longer and longer, and as they sway back and forth, they hook onto bees on the right and left until they form a living curtain.

They hang themselves up like this to produce wax. You see, there are four wax pockets on each side of the bee's abdomen. And after about twenty-four hours of hanging, wax begins to appear from these pockets. When a bee feels its wax is ready, it climbs up over the other bees, takes the wax out of its pockets, chews it, and pats it onto the comb.

At first they just pile on wax. Then they form rough cups, climb into them, and push. And apparently all this pushing sets up vibrations which enable the bees to judge the elasticity and thickness of the walls. The result—the perfect shape and the incredibly thin walls. And that's the way the comb is built. The bees perform their tasks in perfect cooperation, as if their assignments were posted on a bulletin board!

It must be a marvel of organization, you say. Yes. But who directs it?

It is true that no honeybee lives to itself. They all live for the hive. There may be forty to seventy-five thousand bees in a hive, or more, all working in perfect harmony, as a unit.

But who is the leader? Is it the queen? You might say she exerts leadership at the time of swarming. But even then the worker bees play the key role in locating a new nest site. The queen, of course, is an egg-laying machine. In a single day she can lay two thousand eggs. And evidently she does produce chemical signals that in some way enable the colony to function smoothly. For we are told that it takes less than a hundred worker bees to build a comb if the queen is present, but thousands of them if there is no queen. But is she the leader of the hive? Certainly not.

And the drones are not the leaders. These male bees are completely indolent. They spend their lifetime waiting—just waiting for a chance to chase after a queen on her mating flight. The worker bees are unquestionably the real marvels of the hive. But they have no leader. Yet somehow they get all the right things done!

Bees need two things—pollen and nectar. Both are found in flowers. And as they fly off to the fields of flowers, they go marvelously equipped. In the first place, a honeybee is a fantastically engineered flying machine. Man-made freight planes can carry a payload of about 25 percent of their weight. But bees can carry almost 100 percent of their weight. The bee needs no propeller or jet. Its short, wide wings both lift and drive it. It can move straight up or down, or it can hover in midair. Its stubby wings fold in a split second when it dives into a flower. Or it can use its wings as a fan to cool the beehive.

The bee has three places for storing cargo. One is a tank inside its body in which it stores nectar. Then, on its hind legs, it has two storage baskets for carrying pollen. Imagine a freight plane with its load dangling underneath!

Are these pollen baskets something that evolved because of a need? Well, man first wrote about the bee in the year 3000 B.C. It had the pollen baskets then. And it hasn't changed since!

A bee can suck up a load of nectar in a minute. It takes three minutes for it to build up two bulging loads of pollen in the baskets on its hind legs.

How does it do it? Well, the bee dives into a flower, its body picking up pollen by brushing past the pollen boxes. It splashes about in the flower, and the yellow powder clings to the hairs on its body.

But now it isn't so simple. How does it get the pollen into the baskets? And how does it keep the pollen from blowing away in flight? The load must be moistened, pressed together, tamped down, and evenly balanced on each leg. But believe it or not, the bee does it—and all the while hovering in midair or hanging by one claw!

And now the little honeybee, acting as a scout, has discovered a field of flowers and is ready to return to the hive with a sample of the nectar and the pollen. How will it find its way back? Keep in mind that it may be several miles away, and that its search may have led it in several directions before it made its discovery. Yet now it will fly straight back to the hive!

Who told it how to do it? What sort of navigational equipment does it possess? And once back in the hive, how will it communicate to its thousands of fellow bees the location of the treasure it has found?

It is true that bees are able to distinguish odors with great skill. If a bee returns to the hive with nectar from flowers nearby, the other bees will leave the hive and fly directly to the source. And they also act as if they have an internal clock. If they discover that food is available at a particular time of day, they return for more at the same hour the next day.

But what if the flowers are several miles distant? Surely there must be some limitation to the tiny creatures' sense of smell. What then? How can the little bee get across to its fellow bees the location of the treasure it has found?

Well, you haven't heard anything yet. Let me tell you about the "waggle dance"!

Sometimes a bee returning with nectar and pollen goes through a peculiar performance that many scientists believe is its way of communicating the location of the source of nectar. It gives samples of the nectar to the other bees and gets them all excited. Then, as they watch, it does a fancy dance before them—called the waggle dance because of the way it waggles its abdomen. It goes through a figure eight across the face of the comb. And the astonishing thing is that the angle of the dance down the vertical comb represents the horizontal direction of the food source with respect to the direction of the sun.

And not only that. The number of dances per minute indicates the distance to the field. But surprisingly, the number is in reverse ratio to the distance. That is, the farther away the field, the smaller the number. In other words, if the bee goes through ten rounds in fifteen seconds, the field of flowers is three hundred feet away. But if the bee moves in slow motion, say two rounds in fifteen seconds, the flowers are almost four miles away. And listen to this. A little calculation will show that this relationship to distance is not one of simple arithmetic, but is logarithmic! What do you think of that?

What kind of brain does the little honeybee have? Who taught it to do all this? How did this tiny creature learn to relate sun angles and distances to dance-step routines? And how is it that millions of bees understand the language?

Now I am aware that some scientists are not convinced that bees do understand the language. They are not convinced that this strange dance really does communicate to other bees the location of a field of flowers. I am aware of the controversy over this matter.

But if by any chance you are inclined to doubt, then consider this. A bee, by means of this dance, can communicate the location to human beings. Men can understand it. Men can watch the dance and find the field of flowers. Is that any less striking? Is it any less a miracle to communicate that information to human beings, in logarithmic terms, than to get it across to other bees? I think not!

I say again, What kind of brain does the little honeybee have? Is it an accident?

One writer suggests that if you wished to duplicate the internal circuitry of the honeybee, if you wished to match its navigational and guidance system, this is what you would need to start with: "Internal clock. Polarized-light sensor. Sun-angle-azimuth computer. Instrument for measuring true vertical. Dead-reckoning equipment. Wind-speed and direction indicator. Trigonometric calculator and tables. Air- and ground-speed indicators."

It sounds a little extravagant. But is it really—after what we have already seen of the honeybee's accomplishments?

And I wonder if you realize just how necessary the honeybee is—even to life itself. Bees, of course, could not exist without plants and flowers, with their pollen and their nectar. But it works both ways. Many kinds of plants and flowers could not exist without the bees to pollinate them. In fact, many of the most beautiful or most fruitful plants would disappear. And what a loss that would be!

Now tell me. Let's reason again. Did the honeybee, with all its fantastic equipment for its job, just happen? Through long ages? A little bit at a time?

What if the bee started out with no pollen baskets on its hind legs? What if it had the pollen baskets, but not the knee joints to press the pollen into the baskets, or the sense to know how to do it? What if it had no hairs on its body to collect the pollen—or the hairs but no way to comb off the pollen? What if it hadn't developed a nectar tank—yet? What if it had no wax-making equipment—or didn't know it was supposed to hang up in a festoon for twenty-four hours to make the wax come out? What if the wax would not withstand the high temperatures of the hive, as few waxes could? What if the bees didn't know how to make royal jelly to feed the queen—and the queen died? What if a bee couldn't find its way back to the hive—or back to a field of flowers?

The questions fairly tumble out. They are endless. I think you can see that any one piece of the bee's physical equipment might be useless without the others. To be of use, the bee's equipment and know-how would have to have developed simultaneously—not little by little! Or—if evolution happened—consider this. That very first bee, away back there, sitting on a limb of a tree. What kind of bee was it? Was it a queen? But a queen could not reproduce without a drone with which to mate.

Was it a drone? Drones can't reproduce themselves without a queen.

A worker bee, then? Hardly. For worker bees are creatures that can't possibly reproduce themselves.

It is difficult to escape the conclusion that the whole colony would have to evolve at once, simultaneously—with every individual bee's physical equipment and know-how fully developed, ready for business!

And, of course, with the honeybee as with the birds, that isn't evolution at all. That is creation!

Isn't it easier to believe the simple, uncomplicated, straight-forward statement that you find on the first page of your Bible? "In the beginning God created the heaven and the earth."

You may have heard the story of the unbeliever who rescued an orphan boy from a burning building. Having lost his own wife and child, he wanted to adopt the lad. Christian neighbors were skeptical about the wisdom of placing the boy in an infidel home. But the applicant won his case when he held up his hand, badly burned in the rescue of the lad, and said, "I have only one argument. It is this."

He proved to be a good father, and little Jimmy never tired of hearing how Daddy had saved him from the fire. And he liked best to hear about the scarred hand. One day with his new father he visited a display of art masterpieces. One painting interested him especially—the one of Jesus reproving Thomas for his unbelief and holding out His scarred hand.

"Tell me the story of that picture, Daddy," the little fellow pleaded.

"No, not that one."

"Why not?"

"Because I don't believe it."

"But you tell me the story of Jack the giant-killer, and you don't believe that."

So he told him the story. And Jimmy said, "It's like you and me, Daddy." And then he went on, "It wasn't nice of Thomas not to believe after the good Man had died for him. What if they had told me how you saved me from the fire and I had said I didn't believe you did it?"

The father could not escape the sound reasoning of a little child. He had used his own scarred hand to win a small boy's heart. Could he continue to resist the scarred hand of the Man who had died for him—and say He didn't do it? The mightiest argument of all is the cross of Calvary. The scarred hands of Jesus. Hands that were wounded in His encounter with the forces of evil—so that you and I could live! What can we do but fall at His feet and say with Thomas, "My Lord and my God!"

Chapter 4
Fingerprints in Stone

The year 1968 was a bitter pill to swallow. January stormed in with the North Korean capture of the USS *Pueblo* and the shocking Tet Offensive in Vietnam. Springtime cursed us with the assassinations of Martin Luther King and Robert Kennedy. Summer brought no relief as the Vietnam peace talks dragged on and anti-war protests intensified.

No doubt about it, 1968 was a year we would just as soon forget. That is, except for Christmas Eve. A beacon of hope came to us that night, the thrill of accomplishment. For the first time in history men were orbiting the moon. And they were Americans! We could hardly believe our eyes as television relayed the dramatic lunar vista beneath Apollo 8. Astronauts Frank Borman, James Lovell and William Anders sent their Christmas greetings from a quarter million miles away. Then they read to us the first chapter of an old Book. Comforting words, somehow familiar and yet nearly forgotten: "In the beginning God created the heavens and the earth."

The *New York Times,* commenting on that Scripture reading from lunar orbit, observed, "Somehow it was exactly right." Yes, what could have been more appropriate for our astronauts than to recognize that the

blue sphere they looked back upon exists not by accident, but because God put it here?

Some months after the mission of Apollo 8, I
learned of a rather unusual incident that had taken
place that Christmas Eve. Naturally, many reporters
were present at the Space Center in Houston, some of
them from foreign nations. Among them were two
from a country without a Christian background. These
men had been deeply impressed as the astronauts read
from Genesis. The stark splendor of those grand words
touched their minds and hearts.

Not realizing they had been listening to Scripture,
they asked somone from NASA if a script from which
the astronauts read might be available. The American
official replied with a meaningful smile, "Why, yes,
when you get back to your hotel room, just open the
drawer of your nightstand. You will find a book bound
in black. And the script from which the astronauts
read is on the very first page."

"In the beginning God created." Strange as it may
seem, many Christians in America are not as moved
by these immortal words as those atheist journalists
were. Even many churchgoing scientists and edu-
cators, searching for the origins of life, find themselves
unable to accept any answer that points to a Creator.
They would gladly spend millions of dollars probing
outer space to find our roots. They would welcome
some ancient legend or embrace some dusty artifact.
But not the Bible account of Creation!

They seem to enjoy bobbing like corks on the sea of
uncertainty. If they knew something for sure, they
couldn't speculate anymore. All this to escape a
Creator! All this to escape moral responsibility?

I'm convinced that doubting God's Word is not just

a problem of logic. It's more a problem of attitude. Human nature wants to "do its own thing," although we might not want to admit it. So we hide our doubts amid intellectual verbiage.

It was Aldous Huxley who said, "The philosopher who finds no meaning in the world is not concerned exclusively with a problem in pure metaphysics, he is also concerned to prove that there is no valid reason why he personally should not do as he wants to do" (*Ends and Means*, p. 315).

You see, if there is a Creator, then we stand accountable before Him who gave us life. But if we are only sophisticated animals, arriving here by chance, then we have no responsibility. We can do as we please. Or at least whatever we can get away with.

No doubt about it, a God powerful enough to create is unpopular in scientific circles. But lately we hear words of unrest among scientists. Not a few have come to realize that life is too complex to have sprung unannounced from a puddle of chemicals sparked by random lightning bolts. Here and there we find movement toward the Genesis account, what one writer calls "a sheepish resort" to the idea of a Creator. Some scientists now boldly declare their faith in the Bible account of creation. One of them, Robert Gentry, has caused quite a stir among his peers by his discovery of what one evolutionist calls "a tiny mystery."

We will discuss Gentry's fascinating discovery in a moment, but first let me tell you his story.

Bob Gentry had grown up in a Christian home believing the biblical account of life's origins. But while taking a freshman biology course at the University of Florida, he began doubting the Scriptures. By the time he finished his studies there, he had become a theistic evolutionist—one who disbelieves the Genesis creation account but still believes God exists. One day an agnostic friend recommended a television program called "It Is Written." Gentry had no idea religion was involved until he tuned in to our telecast the next Sunday evening. But he then became one of our regular viewers. When I visited Orlando in the spring of 1959 to conduct some lectures, the Gentrys invited me to their home. We discussed creation and evolution. I expressed my conviction that those who discard the account of Genesis also discredit the rest of the Bible. For instance, the Ten Commandments teach beyond question that God created the world in six literal days. We looked at the fourth commandment together:

"Remember the Sabbath day, to keep it holy. Six days you shall labor and do all your work, but the seventh day is the Sabbath of the Lord your God. In it you shall do no work . . . for in six days the Lord made the heavens and the earth. . . . Therefore the Lord blessed the Sabbath day and hallowed it" (Exodus 20:8-11, NKJV).

This Sabbath commandment directly challenged Bob Gentry's confidence in evolution. He had been trying to maintain faith in the Bible by equating the six days of creation with six long geological eras. But now he realized that if such were the case, the commandment would be saying something like this:

"Six billion years you shall labor, and do all your work, but the seventh billion years is the Sabbath of the Lord your God. In it you shall do no work . . . for in six billion years the Lord made heaven and earth . . . and rested the seventh billion years. Therefore the Lord blessed the seventh billion years, and hallowed it."

That gets a little ridiculous, wouldn't you say? Well, Bob Gentry thought so too. So now he had a puzzle to solve. The Sabbath commandment proved that Genesis 1 required six, twenty-four-hour days in the creation week. But science seemed to indicate otherwise—radiometric dating appeared to prove the earth to be billions of years old.

This conflict between Scripture and science caused quite a dilemma for Gentry. At first he thought he must either reject the Bible as unreliable or surrender his belief in science. Instead, he decided to search out the scientific evidence to see for himself if it could be reconciled with the creation account of God's Word.

Gentry began to realize that the case for evolution rested on shaky ground. Everything depended upon a questionable assumption known as the "uniformitarian principle." This theory supposes that the universe evolved through the ages by means of physical laws that have never changed. If evidence could be found disproving this supposed uniformity, the evolutionary theory would fall apart. Geologists would have no basis for assuming that radioactive decay has been constant throughout history, no basis for believing the earth has existed for billions of years. With these thoughts churning in his mind, Bob Gentry moved his family to the Atlanta area. There he taught physics while pursuing graduate studies at the Georgia Institute of Technology. Gentry's quest for truth led him to investigate radioactive halos. (These are imprints of radioactivity in rocks which reveal the radiation present long ago when the earth came into existence.) But the department chairman wasn't enthusiastic about this new area of study. For a year he tried to discourage Gentry.

Finally he said, "Well, look, Bob. The time has come

for me to tell you frankly, if you want to do this research, fine. But you can't do it at Georgia Tech. I don't think you're going to find anything. But what if you did? If you published evidence that disrupted the evolutionary time scale, what would happen to Georgia Tech? You would be an embarrassment to everyone." And so Bob Gentry took his conscience away from Georgia Tech, forfeiting his doctoral dreams under those circumstances. Now, in the summer of 1964, he found himself nearly destitute, without a regular income. The family exhausted their savings as well as funds borrowed from relatives in launching new research into those promising radioactive halos. They were determined to continue this quest for truth, regardless of the consequences.

For the next few months things remained rather bleak for the Gentry family. Nothing much turned up in Bob's research. Then he began noticing under the microscope that certain rocks had unusual ring patterns. These mysterious "radiohalos" showed evidence of radioactivity with a fleeting existence, lasting just a very brief time and then disappearing.

Bob explains it this way: "Suppose I have a glass of water and I put an Alka Seltzer tablet in it. The bubbles flow out and then disappear within just a few seconds. Either I freeze that water instantly and catch the bubbles in transit, or else they're gone forever.

"That's exactly what I was looking at under the microscope. Radioactivity in rapid transition, like those bubbles, had been quickly trapped in earth's foundation rocks. If those rocks had taken hundreds of thousands of years to cool and solidify, as evolutionists believe, these radiohalos could never have been formed. Something with such a fleeting existence must have been trapped in a matter of minutes. But how?"

Finally one spring afternoon in 1965 Bob Gentry received his answer. He tells what happened:

"I was home alone with my three children. The house was silent—it was our "quiet hour," and my boisterous little ones were asleep. I moved my borrowed microscope from the back room to the front of the house to reexamine those fascinating halos.

"Suddenly, as I stared into the microscope, two verses from Scripture flashed into my mind: 'By the word of the Lord were the heavens made; and all the host of them by the breath of his mouth. . . . For he spake, and it was done; he commanded, and it stood fast' (Psalm 33:6, 9).

"As I sat there stunned, a solution suggested itself. *These radiohalos in earth's foundation rocks revealed radiation that had been active long ago but since had ceased. So what most geologists thought would have taken ages could have happened quite quickly. Could this be scientific evidence of an instantaneous creation event? Could these radiohalos, in a sense, be God's fingerprints?*"

Evidently Bob Gentry was onto something here. Something really big!

Gradually he realized the tremendous implications of his discovery. He determined to test his findings by subjecting them to inspection by his peers in the world's most reputable scientific journals. But before anything could be published, it would have to survive cautious and critical analysis. And once in print, the article would be further scrutinized by evolutionists everywhere. Any errors in his methodology would be quickly exposed. Gentry managed to publish more than twenty reports in noted scientific journals. The basic criticism he met was, "This can't be true because evolution is true." But his conclusions remained intact.

Eventually Bob Gentry came to be recognized as the world's foremost authority in his particular sub-specialty. The U.S. Atomic Energy Commission invited him to do research as a guest scientist at the Oak Ridge National Laboratory. October 27, 1981, Gentry was at work in his office at Oak Ridge when the phone rang. The Attorney General's office from the state of Arkansas was calling—they needed Gentry to testify at the forthcoming Arkansas creation trial as one of the expert science witnesses for the state. The teaching of creation in public schools had been opposed by the American Civil Liberties Union as being unscientific. Gentry was asked to meet the challenge by presenting his scientific evidence for creation.

At the trial, Gentry's research was scrutinized again by some of the world's most distinguished evolutionists. Then it came time for the ACLU's geologist to be cross-examined. Asked specifically about the fleeting existence of radioactive halos, he conceded that evolution had no satisfactory explanation for them. The courtroom listened in awe as he could only say, "Gentry has found a tiny mystery which scientists someday will solve."

Yes, the testimony of earth's granite rock halos is creation's tiny mystery. But scientists will never solve it. They will never solve it because the Creator of the universe has placed in those halos His eternal fingerprints. Evidence that cannot be contradicted. Many honest minds these days are becoming convinced about creation because of Bob Gentry. But whether or not we accept his compelling conclusions, one fact remains self-evident: It does matter what we believe about our beginnings. For what we believe about how we got here determines what we believe about God. If He has misled us in the Bible about creation, how can He be a God worth worshiping? And what we believe about our beginnings determines what we believe about the future. For if we discard the book of Genesis as myth and legend, why should we take the prophecies of Revelation seriously?

What we believe about our origin affects what we believe about ourselves; it affects our sense of self-worth. For if we just evolved from some lowly cell in the sea, we would not have the dignity of being formed in the image of God. And if the human race did not fall from that high position, if Adam didn't sin, then why did we need a Saviour for the human race? The mission of Jesus becomes pointless and the cross only a meaningless drama!

We could go on and on. I think you can see that what we believe about our beginnings could well determine our eternal destiny. Is it any wonder that the devil, fighting against our souls, aims his sharpest arrows at the first seven chapters of Genesis?

Why is this generation, obsessed with piecing together our beginnings, looking everywhere but in God's Word? There can be only one answer. It wants to find Adam, but not in Genesis! Yet all the while the simple statement of Scripture stands firm, quietly inviting our faith: "In the beginning God created." Could it be that the evidence collected by Bob Gentry and many others was left by the Creator to help establish faith in the Genesis account? After all, the Bible itself says: "Now faith is the substance of things hoped for, the evidence of things not seen" (Hebrews 11:1, NKJV). Though the Genesis account will never be proven beyond question, God has given all the evidence we need for strong confidence in His creation.

Doubt is in the air. But so are the birds, who fly above us better equipped for navigation than the latest air force fighter jets, able to traverse unmapped oceans with their built-in instruments.

Controversy swirls around us. But so do the bats, who effortlessly operate their ultrasonic radar, reminding us that neither technology nor wisdom are exclusive with the human mind.

Skepticism encircles the earth. But so do the stars, speeding along in their unerring orbits, keeping their appointments with a precision that boggles the mind. Book after book insists authoritatively that this earth evolved over millions of years. Evolutionists talk confidently about the magic of the ages, of happy accidents that exploded us ever upward—with never a need for intelligent direction, never a need for God. But all the while birds and bats and the stars eloquently challenge their entrenched beliefs. Long ago David proclaimed, "The heavens declare the glory of God; and the firmament shows His handiwork. Day unto day utters speech, and night unto night reveals knowledge. There is no speech nor language where their voice is not heard" (Psalm 19:1-3, NKJV).

Nobody can escape the grand harmony as all nature joins in the unmistakable chorus, "There is a Creator!" But the One who made this world also let His creatures nail Him to a rough, splintery cross outside Jerusalem—so that lost sinners might find eternal life in Him. And even the evidence of the birds and the bats, of suns and racing constellations, convincing as it is, pales before the mighty argument of Calvary.